Food is much more than keeping you alive; it is an artistic expression, a celebration and a way to share one's culture. That's why we decided the best way to bring a piece of Syrian culture to you was through these authentic recipes. In Syria, cuisine and hospitality are a much more cherished part of life than in Britain. Whether chatting with a friend or celebrating a festival, food is always at the centre of it all.

These recipes have been written by the three Syrian families now living locally in the Sevenoaks area. Each of these families have played a role in sharing recipes from their region of Syria. They are all supported by the amazing work of the charity Sevenoaks Welcomes Refugees, where the funds from this book will go.

We are a small group of five from Sevenoaks School, and we have been working with Sevenoaks Welcomes Refugees since the start of the 2018/19 academic year. We were motivated to produce this book because we feel strongly about breaking down the cultural barriers that can prevent social integration. We hope to give you a flavour of the culture and the refugees' personalities through these personal and traditional recipes.

Hope you enjoy!

Why this book is in aid of Sevenoaks Welcomes Refugees

Sevenoaks Welcomes Refugees was formed in March 2017. It is comprised of a group of volunteers living in Sevenoaks and the surrounding area who have come together to welcome and help support the Syrian refugees now being re-settled in our community by the UK government, Kent County Council and Sevenoaks District Council. The group is in the process of applying for charitable status.

The refugees have fled from the fighting in Syria, where the conflict that has raged since 2011 has created the worst refugee and displacement crisis of our time. The situation in Syria has been – and continues to be – appalling. Half the country's population has been killed or forced to flee their homes; 5.2 million people have been forced to seek safety in neighbouring countries e.g. Egypt, Lebanon, Jordan, Turkey; 6.3 million people are internally displaced within Syria, and the war is estimated to have killed more than 480,000 people.

Sevenoaks District Council is participating in the official resettlement scheme, Syrian Vulnerable Persons Resettlement Scheme (SVPRS), run by the UK government working closely with the UN High Commissioner for Refugees (UNHCR). Those under the scheme desperately need assistance. It prioritises those who cannot be supported effectively in their region of origin: including women and children at risk, people in severe need of medical care, and survivors of torture and violence. The UK government has committed to bringing 20,000 refugees to the UK under this scheme by 2020. A further 3,000 people (vulnerable children with their families) were included under the Vulnerable Children's Resettlement Scheme in 2017.

Refugees or asylum seekers that have made their way across Europe are not part of this scheme. People in the scheme are given five years of Humanitarian Protection. The UK government sets the criteria and UNHCR identifies potential cases. The final decision on who comes to the UK rests with the government.

The SVPRS is administered across Kent by Kent County Council and in our area by Sevenoaks District Council. Professional support for the families is provided by Clarion, who are contracted by KCC to work closely with the families, ensuring that they can access all the relevant services, benefits and other help they are entitled to. Each family is provided with a key worker who will work intensively with them for the first year, and continues to support afterwards when needed but on a gradually reducing scale, depending on individual need.

How Funds Raised Will Be Spent

Sevenoaks Welcomes Refugees (SWR) volunteers provide local practical support to refugee families in our area, helping them settle into our community having fled the fighting in Syria. Their support includes welcoming and befriending, help with learning English, finding jobs, providing lifts, and sourcing necessary household items. They help the refugees connect with local community groups (e.g. allotment society, running group, dance circle, art society) and organise social events. Volunteers also help find private landlords willing to take part in the rental scheme.

Sevenoaks Welcomes Refugees makes grants to refugee families to assist in their long-term resettlement and improve their quality of life. From warm clothes and children's swimming lessons to laptops, professional accountancy exams, English language books and travel costs for outings, these small grants are helping all the families thrive in a new country. All family members can suggest what they would find useful.

The group aims not to spend money on things that could either be provided by the SVPR scheme or be found second-hand through requests to its supporters. Some money is spent on raising awareness, funds and recruiting more volunteers to help with the language support programme and our 'family teams'. They are all volunteers.

SWR is also looking at how it can contribute its funds to enable more local properties to be rented to refugee families. Finding ways to reduce the gap between market levels and the rent available from the scheme will mean it can help resettle some more of the 20,000 Syrian refugees the UK has pledged to help, who are currently living in wretched conditions in the countries surrounding Syria: Egypt, Lebanon, Jordan and Turkey.

The families resettling here live either in private rented accommodation (paid for by the scheme) or in the council's own social housing. They receive benefits and can work from the day they arrive. Since July 2017, three refugee families have arrived in the Sevenoaks area under this scheme: one in Eynsford, one in Swanley, and most recently a third family in Sevenoaks town.

If you'd like to help support refugees from Syria now living in our community, or know more about what the local refugee support group is doing, please contact Humphrey Pring, chair of Sevenoaks Welcomes Refugees at sevenoakswelcomesrefugees@gmail.com.

We want to start by thanking Sevenoaks School for providing us with this valuable opportunity to collaborate with Sevenoaks Welcomes Refugees. Thank you Mrs Henshaw and Mrs Featherstone - the project would not have come to fruition without your tremendous support.

We also wish to thank Humphrey, Tracey, and everyone at Sevenoaks Welcomes Refugees for inspiring us to embark on this project and making it possible by facilitating our connections with the families.

Our enormous thanks to all our Syrian friends who worked with us on this book. It was great to get to know you in our meetings at Sevenoaks School and in your homes over the last few months. Thank you so much for sharing the delicious recipes with us and bringing the taste of Damascus, Idlib and Aleppo to Sevenoaks. We wish you well with your resettlement in our community as you begin to build new futures for your families here in Sevenoaks, Eynsford and Swanley. It is a pleasure to see you use your energy, skills and experience as mothers, fathers, chefs, financial managers, general managers, shoemakers and artists. Special thanks to Khalid, Mona, Mohammad, Kharia, Rasha, and Bushra for their help with this project. We would have no recipes without you!

We would like to express our huge appreciation to the volunteers who gave their time to translate and transcribe the recipes (and their cultural significance) from Arabic into English: Violette (our great coordinator), Claire, Jeremy, Michael and Zeina. Also to Janet for suggesting the idea of a recipe book.

The photographs in this book are either taken by Ethan Brown or provided by the refugee families themselves. We want to thank Mr Merewether for editing the images and giving us expert guidance on the design of the book. All the paintings in this book are done by Mohammad. Thank you for sharing your incredible talents with us.

Sevenoaks student, Gwendolyn Liu, has found the time, in amongst a rigorous IB Diploma course, to put the whole book together. Her dogged determination and stellar levels of organisation and coordination cannot be rivalled.

Love,

"A Taste of Home" Team
Gwendolyn Liu
Anna Power
Ethan Brown
Eesha Singh
Oscar Petter

TABLE OF CONTENTS

Red Lentil Soup

Ingredients

250 g red lentils, rinsed
1 litre water
2 chicken stock cubes
1 tbsp (15 ml) lemon juice
1 tsp ground cumin
1/2 tsp dried coriander leaf
1/2 tsp paprika
1 tbsp (15 g) butter
3 garlic cloves, crushed
salt, to taste

What To Do

1. Add the lentils and water to a medium-sized saucepan. Bring to the boil over medium-high heat.

2. Cover and cook for 10 minutes on high heat, skimming off any froth that rises to the top.

3. Add the chicken stock cubes, lemon juice, cumin, coriander and paprika. Reduce the heat to a simmer, cover and cook for a further 30 minutes.

4. While you wait, melt the butter in a small saucepan over medium heat. Add the crushed garlic and gently fry for a few minutes, or until lightly browned. Be careful not to over-brown the garlic as it will go bitter.

5. Add the garlic to the lentil soup, season to taste with salt and stir.

Spring Salad

Ingredients

2 medium vine tomatoes, finely diced
1 iceberg lettuce, roughly chopped
1/2 cucumber, finely diced
1 green bell pepper, finely diced
1 tbsp dried mint
2 tbsp (30 ml) extra virgin olive oil
1 tbsp (15 ml) fresh lemon juice
salt, to taste

What To Do

1. Add the tomatoes, lettuce, cucumber, bell pepper and mint to a serving bowl and toss to thoroughly combine.

2. Whisk together the olive oil, lemon juice and salt in a separate bowl.

3. Drizzle the dressing over the salad just before serving.

Syrian Fattoush Salad

"This is a light dish that we consider a kind of salad but includes roasted bread. My family loves to eat it a few times a week. We eat it with each other and with good friends too. It is nice for days when it is hot outside and we don't feel very hungry and also perfect for having with other dishes for a larger meal."

Ingredients

2 pitta breads, khobez or any flatbread
3 medium tomatoes, roughly chopped
3 medium cucumbers, roughly chopped
1 medium lettuce (any type), roughly chopped
1 onion, finely sliced
6 medium radishes, finely sliced
1 bunch mint, roughly chopped
1 bunch parsley, roughly chopped
1 bunch purslane, roughly chopped
1 tsp sumac (this can be generous)

For the dressing

1/2 cup (125 ml) olive oil
1/4 cup (60 ml) fresh lemon juice
1 tbsp (15 ml) red wine or cider vinegar
5 cloves garlic, crushed
salt, to taste

What To Do

1. Brush the bread with a little olive oil and toast on both sides in a hot oven for 10 - 12 minutes, or until well browned. Rip into pieces.

2. Add the tomatoes, cucumbers, lettuce, onion, radishes, mint, parsley and purslane to a large serving bowl. Toss to combine.

3. In a small bowl whisk together the olive oil, lemon juice, vinegar, garlic and salt.

4. Add half of the toasted bread to the vegetable salad and toss to combine.

5. Just before serving, pour the dressing over the salad and toss well.

6. Scatter the remaining toasted bread pieces over the salad and sprinkle with sumac.

Aubergine Salad with Yoghurt & Flatbread

"This delicious dish is one of the most popular dishes that we use as a side dish with lots of other main meals and when we BBQ. When we gather with family or friends, someone always brings this to the occasion. It is very tasty and healthy. I learned to make this salad with my Aunt who was a very good cook. I still think of her when I make it."

Ingredients

olive oil for frying
2 medium aubergines, sliced
1 flatbread

For the yoghurt sauce

2 cups (500 ml) plain yoghurt
juice of 1 lemon
2 tbsp (30 ml) extra virgin olive oil
1 clove garlic, crushed
salt and black pepper to taste

To garnish

1 handful pine kernels (optional)
fresh parsley, finely chopped
fresh mint, finely chopped

What To Do

1. Line a plate with kitchen paper towel and set aside.

2. In a large skillet or frying pan over medium-high heat, warm the olive oil. Fry the aubergine rounds, in batches, until golden brown on both sides. Transfer to the kitchen paper towel-lined plate to absorb excess oil. Set aside.

3. Fry the flatbread until golden brown on both sides. Transfer to a kitchen paper towel-lined plate to absorb excess oil. Once the excess oil has been absorbed chop into pieces. Set aside

4. In a large bowl thoroughly mix together the yoghurt, lemon juice, 2 tablespoons olive oil, garlic, salt and pepper.

5. Lay the aubergine rounds on a serving dish and cover with the yoghurt sauce and then the chopped flatbread pieces.

6. To serve scatter with pine nuts (optional) and the parsley and mint.

Tabouli (Tabbouleh) Salad

"This salad is ideal for hot summer days. It is very nutritious and light. We always eat it when going for a picnic. That is one reason it is one of my favorite meals. It always makes me think of good times."

Ingredients

2 tbsp (about 20 g) fine bulgur wheat
2 bunches flat leaf parsley, finely chopped
2 cups (50 g) fresh mint, finely chopped
4 medium vine tomatoes, finely diced
1 medium brown onion, finely diced
1/2 cucumber, finely diced
2 spring onions, finely sliced
1 small lettuce (any kind), finely sliced
2 tbsp (30 ml) lemon juice
2 tbsp (30 ml) olive oil
salt, to taste

What To Do

1. Place the bulgur in a fine mesh sieve and rinse. Transfer to a large bowl.

2. Add enough boiling water to cover and soak for 5 minutes. Drain and return the bulgur to the bowl.

3. Add all the chopped vegetables and herbs to the bulgur and toss together.

4. In a bowl whisk together the lemon juice, olive oil and salt.

5. Just before serving pour over the dressing and toss again.

Damascene Fattet Hummus

"We only eat this dish at breakfast. It's very delicious but quite filling. There are many different ways this dish can be made. The recipe in this book is the best one for me because it is how my family like it. When we start our day with Damascene Fattet Hummus, we know it is going to be a good and productive day."

Ingredients

1 kg dry chickpeas
Alternative: 5 (400 g) cans chickpeas
5 tbsp full-fat plain yoghurt
3 tbsp tahini (sesame paste)
juice of 1 lemon
2 cloves garlic, crushed
1 tsp cumin
1 tsp salt, or to taste
2 pitta breads, khobez or any flatbread
1 tsp sweet paprika
pinch black pepper
4 tbsp (60 g) ghee (clarified butter) or olive oil
mixed nuts and/or pine nuts
2 tbsp chopped parsley

What To Do

1. Dry chickpeas need about 12 hours soaking in cold water before cooking. A quicker method is to use canned chickpeas.

2. Method 1 using dry chickpeas: add the soaked chickpeas to a large pot of water and gently boil for about 45 – 60 minutes, or until soft. Drain the chickpeas but reserve the cooking water.

3. Method 2 using canned chickpeas: empty the cans into a pot on medium heat and warm the chickpeas. Drain the chickpeas but reserve the liquid.

4. In a large bowl mash half of the chickpeas. Add the yoghurt, tahini, lemon juice, garlic, cumin and salt. Mix well.

5. To warm up the remaining chickpeas, add to a pot, cover them with the reserved chickpea cooking liquid and warm the chickpeas. Drain and reserve the liquid for soaking the bread.

6. Add a little ghee or olive oil to a pan on medium-high heat and toast the bread on both sides. Cut the bread into pieces and place in a serving dish. Pour a little of the reserved chickpea liquid over the bread pieces and set aside for a short while until the liquid has been absorbed.

7. Add half of the mashed chickpea mixture to the bread and stir well.

8. Add a layer of whole chickpeas and then the rest of the mashed chickpea mixture. Sprinkle with black pepper and paprika.

9. In a small pan set over medium heat melt the ghee or warm the olive oil. Add the mixed nuts and (optional) pine nuts and toast for a few minutes, or until lightly browned, stirring regularly. Remove from the heat and stir in the parsley.

10. Pour over the Hummus chickpea mixture and serve immediately.

Baba Ganoush

Ingredients

2 large aubergines
1 cup (250ml) plain yoghurt
1 cup (130 g) tahini
1 cup (60 ml) lemon juice
3 tbsp chopped parsley
2 tbsp pomegranate molasses
1 tsp salt, to taste
black pepper, to taste
chilli powder or flakes (optional)
1 tbsp (15 ml) extra virgin olive oil
pitta breads, khobez or any flatbread

What To Do

1. Preheat the oven to 180° C.

2. Arrange the aubergines on a lightly oiled baking tray and roast in the oven for 15 - 20 minutes, or until the skin cracks and the aubergine is soft.

3. Set them aside to cool, about 5 minutes. When the aubergines are cool enough to handle cut them in half lengthwise. Either peel the skin off or alternatively scrape the flesh from the skin, whichever method you find easiest.

4. Mash the aubergine with a fork, or a food processor, to a coarse texture. Remove from the food-processor.

5. Add the yoghurt, tahini, lemon juice, parsley and 2 tablespoons of pomegranate molasses to a food-processor and pulse several times to combine. Remove the mixture to a bowl.

6. Add the mashed aubergine to the above mixture and mix together well.

7. Season with salt, black pepper and (optional) chilli.

8. Spoon the mixture onto a serving plate and drizzle with olive oil and pomegranate molasses.

9. Serve with pitta, khobez or flatbread.

Pogaca Rolls

"These rolls are not typical of Syrian cuisine but are widely eaten in Turkey and are sold in bakeries there. They are good anytime, but I especially like them served warm for breakfast. I usually leave the dough to rise overnight so they are ready to bake the next morning. Pogaca rolls freeze well. They will also last up to one week at room temperature if kept in an airtight container."

Ingredients

1 teacup (125 ml) warm water
15g instant dried yeast
1 teacup (125 ml) warm milk
1 teacup (125 ml) sunflower oil
2 medium eggs, lightly beaten
4 tsp (20 g) sugar
5 - 6 teacups (625 g – 750 g) self-raising flour
egg yolks, beaten (for brushing)
nigella or sesame seeds, for garnish (optional)

Filling (optional):

eggs, grated cheese, parsley or other fresh herbs, or chocolate chips.

What To Do

1. In a bowl or glass jug add the warm water (about 40° C not warmer, otherwise it will kill the yeast) and dissolve 1 teaspoon of the sugar. Stir in the yeast and set aside for the yeast to activate. After a few minutes bubbles should appear on the surface of the liquid. This means the yeast is active. If there is no activity it means the yeast is no longer viable and should be discarded. Start again with new yeast. It's always best to test the yeast.

2. Add the yeast mixture, remaining sugar, warm milk, oil and eggs to a large bowl and stir to mix well.

3. Slowly add flour, mixing with the handle of a wooden spoon or your hands, until the mixture has a dough-like consistency. Cover the bowl with a tea towel or plastic wrap and set aside in a warm, draught-free place to rise for at least 5 hours.

4. Preheat the oven to 200°C.

5. After the dough has risen, divide the dough into small egg-sized balls and place them onto a lightly greased baking sheet (leave enough space between the rolls to allow for expansion).

6. If you are using a filling, use your thumbs to make an opening in each roll, add a bit of filling, and then pinch the dough closed to seal it.

7. Brush each ball with beaten egg yolk and (optional) sprinkle with sesame or nigella seeds.

8. Place the baking sheet(s) in the oven and bake for about 10 minutes, or until golden brown.

Megadra with Bulgur

"Megadra is a very old vegetarian dish. It is very famous in Syria, Lebanon and Egypt although has different names in each country. It is a dish my entire family love from my cousins to my aunts and uncles. It is very good."

Ingredients

4 onions (3 halved and sliced, 1 finely diced)
1/2 cup (125 ml) canola or olive oil
2 cups (500 g) red lentils
1 and 1/2 cups (340 g) coarse bulgur wheat
1 tbsp salt, or to taste
black pepper, to taste

What To Do

1. Heat the oil in a frying pan on medium heat and add the sliced onions. Fry the onions, stirring occasionally, until the onions are well caramelised and golden brown. This can take anything from 10 – 20 minutes. Remove the onions from the pan with a slotted spoon and set aside. Reserve the oil in the pan.

2. Add the lentils to a large saucepan and cover with water. Bring to the boil and cook for about 15 minutes, or until almost becoming soft but not cooked through. Drain the lentils, reserving the cooking water. Sprinkle the salt over the lentils and mix well.

3. Add the reserved oil from frying the sliced onion to the large saucepan and sauté the diced onions until soft. Add the par-cooked lentils and bulgur wheat to the onions. Add 500 ml of the reserved lentil cooking water. Bring to the boil and then reduce the heat, cover and simmer for about 10 - 15 minutes, or until the bulgur wheat is done. Stir occasionally. If needed add a little more reserved cooking water. Season with black pepper and salt if desired.

4. Transfer to a serving dish and garnish with the caramelised onion.

5. Serve with yoghurt salad.

Kibbeh

"My mum taught me how to make kibbeh using my hands instead of using a food processor. I have always felt happy about learning how to do that. I will teach my daughter too."

Ingredients

For the outer shell dough

1kg bulgur wheat
1kg brown onion, quartered
1/2 kg minced lamb
salt, to taste
black pepper, to taste
2 tsp cumin
zest of 1 lemon
vegetable oil for deep-frying

Ingredients for the filling

1kg minced lamb or beef
4 brown onions, finely diced
2 tsp cumin
1/2 tsp ground allspice
150 g pine nuts or chopped walnuts
salt. to taste
black pepper, to taste
1 red chilli, finely diced
2 tbsp pomegranate juice or seeds (optional)
zest of 1 lemon

What To Do

To make the outer shell

1. Soak the bulgur wheat in warm water for 30 minutes. Drain and place the bulgur in the centre of a cloth. Wrap up and twist to squeeze out excess water.

2. Add the onion, lamb, salt, pepper, cumin and lemon zest to the bowl of a food-processor and process until it almost becomes a paste.

3. Transfer to a bowl and add the bulgur wheat. Use damp hands to combine the mixture to form a dough.

4. Cover and place in the fridge.

To make the filling

5. Add olive oil to a pan on medium heat and sauté the onions until soft, and then add the meat. Increase the heat to medium-high and brown the meat, stirring occasionally. Remove from the heat.

6. Lightly toast the pine nuts or walnuts in a dry pan until lightly browned.

7. Mix all the ingredients together in a bowl.

To make the kibbeh (makes about 80)

8. It's best to work with damp hands to stop the mixture sticking.

9. Take about 2 tablespoons of outer shell dough and form a ball. Flatten the ball in the palm of your hand to form a disc.

10. Place about 1 tablespoon of filling in the centre of the disc and gently close to form a ball, making sure that the edges of the dough are sealed.

11. Gently shape into an oval with pointed ends that resembles a lemon.

12. Place on a baking tray lined with parchment paper.

13. Dampen your hands again and repeat until you have used all the mixture.

14. Chill for 30 – 60 minutes before frying.

Frying the kibbeh

15. Heat the oil in a large deep-frying pan to 180° C.

16. Deep-fry the kibbeh, in batches, until nicely browned, about 5 minutes. Do not overcrowd the pan as the temperature of the oil will drop too much and the kibbeh will be greasy.

17. Remove with a slotted spoon and place on kitchen paper to drain excess oil.

18. Repeat until you have fried all the kibbeh.

Stuffed Courgettes

"This is a wonderful Turkish dish that is now popular in Middle Eastern countries and all around the world."

Ingredients

For the stock

1 1/2 litre warm water (or chicken stock)
3 tbsp (45 g) tomato paste
1 tbsp (15 g) butter
6 – 8 cloves garlic, finely sliced
3 tbsp (45 ml) tamarind paste
1 tbsp dried mint
salt, to taste
black pepper, to taste

For the stuffed courgette

12 small courgettes (or 6 large, halved)
1 cup (250 g) rice
1/2 cup (125 ml) warm water
1 medium red onion, finely diced
1/4 kg minced beef or lamb
3 tbsp (45 ml) vegetable oil
1 tsp cumin seeds
1 tsp saffron powder
salt and black pepper, to taste

What To Do

1. In a large bowl, dissolve the sugar and the yeast in the warm water. Stir vigorously. Set aside for 5 minutes.

2. Add the flour and the salt to the mixture and beat until it forms a dough – the handle of a large wooden spoon is good for this. Knead the dough using your hands until the dough is smooth and even. Cover and set aside for about 10 minutes.

3. Form small balls from the dough, place on a baking tray lined with parchment paper and cover loosely with plastic wrap. Set aside to rest for 10 minutes.

4. Heat the oil in a frying pan and add the onions and garlic. Sauté until the onions are soft. Add the tomatoes, chilli sauce (or chilli powder), cumin, and salt and pepper to taste and mix together. Cook for a further 10 – 15 minutes over low heat, or until the sauce has thickened. Set aside to cool completely.

5. Dust a large board or a clean counter top with flour. Roll each dough ball into an oval shape. Trim with a sharp knife if necessary. Put about one tablespoon of the filling just off-centre onto each piece of dough. Bring the opposite edge over and seal the edge using your fingertips - it helps to dampen the edge with a little water. Place on a lightly oiled baking tray.

6. Brush the upper surface of the pies with beaten egg, being careful not to get egg-wash on the tray – the pies will stick to the tray!

7. Preheat the oven to 200°C.

8. Bake for 15 to 20 minutes, or until the pies are golden brown.

Spicy Pies

Ingredients

For the dough

1 1/2 cups (375 ml) warm water
2 tbsp (25 g) sugar
1 tbsp (10 g) dry yeast
3 1/2 cups (370 g) plain flour
1 tsp (5 g) salt
1 egg, beaten with a little water

For the filling

5 tbsp (75 ml) olive oil
2 onions, finely diced
2 cloves garlic, crushed
5 tomatoes, skinned and finely diced
2 tbsp (30 ml) hot chilli sauce (or chilli powder)
1/2 - 1 tsp cumin, to taste
salt and black pepper, to taste

What To Do

1. In a large bowl, dissolve the sugar and the yeast in the warm water. Stir vigorously. Set aside for 5 minutes.

2. Add the flour and the salt to the mixture and beat until it forms a dough – the handle of a large wooden spoon is good for this. Knead the dough using your hands until the dough is smooth and even. Cover and set aside for about 10 minutes.

3. Form small balls from the dough, place on a baking tray lined with parchment paper and cover loosely with plastic wrap. Set aside to rest for 10 minutes.

4. Heat the oil in a frying pan and add the onions and garlic. Sauté until the onions are soft. Add the tomatoes, chilli sauce (or chilli powder), cumin, and salt and pepper to taste and mix together. Cook for a further 10 – 15 minutes over low heat, or until the sauce has thickened. Set aside to cool completely.

5. Dust a large board or a clean counter top with flour. Roll each dough ball into an oval shape. Trim with a sharp knife if necessary. Put about one tablespoon of the filling just off-centre onto each piece of dough. Bring the opposite edge over and seal the edge using your fingertips - it helps to dampen the edge with a little water. Place on a lightly oiled baking tray.

6. Brush the upper surface of the pies with beaten egg, being careful not to get egg-wash on the tray – the pies will stick to the tray!

7. Preheat the oven to 200°C.

8. Bake for 15 to 20 minutes, or until the pies are golden brown.

Syrian Omelette

Ingredients

6 medium eggs
1 onion, finely diced
1 small bunch parsley, finely chopped
1 tbsp dried mint
1 clove garlic, crushed
1/4 cup (65 ml) milk
salt and black pepper, to taste
1 tbsp (15 ml) vegetable oil

What To Do

1. Beat the eggs and mix in the onion, parsley, mint, garlic and milk.

2. Season with salt and black pepper.

3. Warm a little oil in a large pan over a medium-high heat.

4. Spoon in enough of the egg mixture to cover the pan and cook for 20- 40 seconds, or until the bottom is browned. Flip the omelette to cook the other side. Slide the omelette onto a plate.

5. Repeat until all the mixture has been used.

6. Serve immediately.

Syrian Moussaka

"Moussaka was originally a Greek dish that has been adapted into Middle Eastern cooking in many different ways. I have a special way of preparing it which has become a tradition in my family. I really enjoy making it as I find the process relaxing and peaceful."

Ingredients

2 tbsp (30 ml) vegetable oil
1 medium brown onion, diced
1 green bell pepper, diced
2 cloves garlic, crushed
1 cup (about 225 g) minced lamb or beef
1 tsp turmeric
salt and black pepper, to taste
2 aubergines, roughly diced
1 medium tomato, chopped
parsley, finely chopped

What To Do

1. Heat the vegetable oil in a large pan or skillet over medium heat. Add the onions and green bell pepper, and sauté until softened, about 10 minutes. Add the garlic and minced lamb or beef and sauté, stirring until the meat is browned.

2. Add the turmeric and season with salt and pepper to taste. Mix in the aubergines and cook over low heat until the aubergine has cooked through, about 15 minutes. Add the tomatoes and stir well. Continue simmering until all the ingredients are cooked through and well combined.

3. Garnish with finely chopped parsley.

Chicken with Potatoes

"This is a nice and easy casserole dish, especially when we have guests. We always can get chicken and potatoes to feed our guests. This is a good meal to share together with friends and family."

Ingredients

2 kg whole chicken (or bone-in, skin-on chicken pieces)
1 1/2 kg potatoes
1 kg tomatoes
salt and black pepper, to taste
1 aubergine and 3 mixed bell peppers, diced (optional)
pitta breads, khobez or any flatbread

For the spice marinade

1 tsp salt, or to taste
1 tsp chilli powder, or to taste
2 tsp dried oregano
1 tsp freshly ground black pepper
1/2 tsp ground ginger
6 cloves garlic, crushed
4 tbsp (60 ml) olive oil

For the yoghurt dip

500 ml plain yoghurt
juice of 1 lemon
2 – 3 cloves garlic, crushed, to taste

What To Do

1. Add all the spice marinade ingredients to a large bowl and mix together well.

2. Cut chicken into portions (if necessary). Add to the spice marinade and thoroughly coat the chicken with the marinade. Cover and place in the fridge for at least 1 hour.

3. Wash and peel the potatoes. Cut into 1 cm-thick slices.

4. Cut the tomatoes into 1 cm-thick slices.

5. Pre-heat the oven to 200°C (or 180°C fan assisted oven).

6. In a large roasting pan add 2 layers of potato and tomato. Alternating with a slice of potato and then a slice of tomato, overlapping slightly. Season with salt and pepper and then add another layer. Optional: if using aubergine and bell peppers, then scatter them evenly over the first potato & tomato layer before adding the second layer. Don't forget to season the aubergines and bell peppers. Pour about 60 ml of water into the roasting pan. The steam will help cook the potatoes.

7. Place the chicken skin-side down on top of the vegetables and drizzle over any remaining marinade.

8. Roast in the oven for 60 – 80 minutes, or until the chicken is cooked (test with a kitchen thermometer probe, the temperature at the thickest part should be 65° C). Turn the chicken over half way through and finish roasting.

9. Make the yoghurt dip by combining in a bowl the yoghurt, lemon juice and garlic. It's best to make this ahead as the flavours blend nicely with a bit of time.

10. Serve with a salad, flatbread and the yoghurt dip.

El Oozy

"This is a very rich and filling dish. It is used a lot at different occasions like weddings and other celebrations. I have always been very good at making this dish and in my younger days, made it for family members' weddings."

Ingredients

4 tbsp (60 ml) vegetable or olive oil
1/2 tsp black pepper
1/2 tsp ground cardamom
1/2 tsp ground cinnamon
1/4 tsp ground turmeric
2 cups (500 g) basmati rice
250 g minced beef or lamb
2 medium carrots, small dice
1 medium onion, small dice
1 cup (160 g) peas (frozen is fine)
8 pieces puff pastry, about 14 cm diameter
1/2 tsp salt
1/4 cup (50 g) roasted almonds, roughly chopped
1 egg, beaten

What To Do

1. Cook the rice according to the package instructions until almost done. Drain, add to a large bowl and set aside to cool.

2. In a large saucepan on medium heat warm the oil. Add the pepper, cardamom, cinnamon and turmeric. Add the minced meat and sauté, stirring, until browned. Add the onions, carrots, peas and salt, and cook on a low heat until the carrots are softened. Stir occasionally. Add the minced meat mixture and half the almonds to the rice and mix together. Set aside to cool.

3. Pre-heat the oven to 160° C.

4. Grease a baking tray lightly with oil. You may need 2 trays for this.

5. Place a piece of puff pastry on the tray and top with 3 tablespoons of the rice mixture just off-centre. Brush the edge of the pastry lightly with water. Fold the pastry over and press the edges together to seal. Repeat with the remaining 7 puff pastry pieces. Brush the tops of the pastries with beaten egg, being careful not to get any on the tray, else the pastries will stick to the tray!

6. Bake in the preheated oven for 35 minutes, or until they are golden brown.

7. Remove to a serving dish and sprinkle with the remaining roasted almonds.

Tabakh Roho

Ingredients

For the Lamb

1 tbsp (15 g) ghee or olive oil
1/2 kg lamb, cut into small pieces
1 tsp Arabic 7 spices mix (see below)
1/2 tsp garlic, crushed

For the Vegetables

2 medium brown onions, diced
1 kg tomatoes, diced
1/2 kg courgettes, diced
1 tbsp (16 g) tomato paste
1/4 (65 ml) cup water
salt, to taste
6 cloves garlic, crushed
3 tsp dried mint

To make the Arabic spice blend

1 tsp paprika
1 tsp ground cumin
1/2 tsp ground coriander seed
1/2 tsp ground cloves
1/2 tsp ground nutmeg
1/2 tsp ground cinnamon
1/4 tsp ground cardamom

What To Do

1. In a pan set over medium heat, melt the ghee. Add the lamb and sauté, stirring, until it is well browned. Add the 7 spices, 1/2 teaspoon crushed garlic and mix well.

2. Add onion, courgette and tomato to the lamb. Stir to combine.

3. In a small bowl, mix the tomato paste, water and salt. Pour over the lamb and vegetable mix. Bring to the boil and then reduce the heat to a simmer. Cook covered for 1 hour.

4. In a small bowl, combine the 6 cloves crushed garlic and dried mint. Add 2 tablespoons of the tomato paste liquid from the pan to the bowl, stir well, and then add to the pan.

5. Cook for another 5 minutes.

Okra with Lamb

"Okra is a summer vegetable that is very healthy and tastes very nice with lamb. The lamb is a stronger flavour so the two mix well. Sometimes we have raised our own lamb that we eat in this dish. When we do that, we invite others over to share in our good fortune."

Ingredients

2 tsp (30 ml) olive oil
1 medium brown onion, sliced
1/4 kg lamb pieces
3 garlic cloves, crushed
1 tsp dried coriander
1/2 kg fresh or frozen small okra
1 tbsp (15 ml) lemon juice
1 tsp salt, or to taste
1 tsp paprika
2 cups (500 ml) water
cooked long grain rice for serving

What To Do

1. In a medium pan with a lid over medium heat, warm the oil. Add the onion, lamb, garlic and coriander, and cook for about 10 minutes, stirring well to stop it sticking to the pan.

2. Add the okra, lemon juice, salt and paprika and stir. Add the water.

3. Cover with the lid, reduce the heat to a simmer, and cook for 30 minutes if using fresh okra, or for 45 minutes if using frozen okra.

4. Serve with cooked rice.

Stuffed Vine Leaves

"This dish takes more time to prepare than any other dish. For this reason, we only make it for special family occasions and festivals. The women in the family enjoy making this dish together. We talk and laugh and have a nice time and then feel very good about serving it because it is made with love."

Ingredients

1/2 kg long grain rice
1/2 kg minced beef
2 tbsp (30 ml) olive oil
4 cloves garlic, crushed
1 tsp dried mint
salt, to taste
freshly ground black pepper,
to taste
1 kg tinned large vine leaves in
brine
juice of 1 lemon

What To Do

1. Cook the rice as per the instructions on the pack. Drain and set aside to cool.

2. In a large bowl mix together the rice, minced meat, olive oil, garlic, mint, salt and pepper.

3. Bring a pot of water to the boil. Remove from the heat, add the vine leaves, and blanch for about 5 minutes to soften and remove some of the salt. Drain and dry on a clean tea towel.

4. Spread a leaf open on a work surface and put 1 1/2 teaspoons of the filling mixture in the middle of the leaf. Fold both sides of the leaf over the stuffing then roll it to close.

5. In a medium-sized saucepan, arrange the stuffed leaves in rows. Add enough boiling water to cover. Carefully place a small, heat-proof plate on top the leaves to keep them submerged in the liquid and then cover the pan with a lid.

6. Cook over low heat for 1 1/2 hours.

7. When the stuffed vine leaves are cooked, carefully remove the plate and add the lemon juice. Remove from the pan and drain off any excess water.

8. Serve hot or cold.

Maqluba (Chicken & Aubergine)

"This is a traditional Syrian dish that is loved by many people. It is like an upside-down tower when it is turned over. There is a myth about the dish that tells of a woman warning the city of its destruction. The city didn't take heed and was turned upside-down. The word maqluba even means upside-down in Arabic."

Ingredients

1 1/2 kg whole chicken
500g good quality long grain rice
2 aubergines, sliced in 1 cm rounds
1 tbsp (15 ml) olive oil
1/2 tsp salt, or to taste
1 tsp black pepper
1 tsp allspice
1 tsp cinnamon
1 tsp turmeric
1/4 cup (50 g) almonds, pistachio or pine nuts

What To Do

1. Boil the chicken in lightly salted water for an hour. Drain and set aside to cool. When it is cool enough de-bone the chicken into pieces but keep the skin on. Reserve the cooking water.

2. Preheat the oven to 180° C.

3. Brush the aubergine slices on both sides with olive oil and arrange them on a baking tray. Roast in the preheated oven until softened.

4. In a large pan with lid, arrange a layer of aubergine rounds, then a layer of rice, then a layer of de-boned chicken. Repeat with another two or three layers again, or until all the ingredients have been used up.

5. Season a litre of the chicken cooking water with the salt (to taste), pepper, allspice, cinnamon and turmeric, and bring to a boil. Pour over the maqluba in the pan.

6. Cover the pan with a lid and cook for 45 minutes over low heat.

7. In the mean-time fry the nuts in a little olive oil until lightly browned.

8. When the maqluba is cooked through remove the lid. Take a round serving dish that is just smaller than the rim of the pan and place it over the maqluba in the pan. Carefully but quickly flip the pan over, holding both the plate and the pan handle firmly. Now lift the pan off with care and the maqluba has been transferred to the serving plate!

9. To serve scatter with the nuts.

Molokhia

"Molokhia is perfect for the summer season when it is fresh. There are many stories about this dish that my family enjoys sharing together when we eat it. My grandmother and her mother made the dish together often. My father used to tell us the stories of how he ate it with his mother and grandmother. The dish is very dear to my heart. When I taste it, I remember the stories."

Ingredients

1 tbsp (15 g) butter
1 head garlic, cloves separated and crushed
1 tsp dried coriander
1 kg Molokhia dried leaves
1 1/2 kg chicken
2 tbsp (30 ml) fresh lemon juice
salt, to taste
black pepper, to taste
2 tsp paprika

What To Do

1. Soak the Molokhia leaves in water for about 2 hours. Drain and rinse in fresh water. Squeeze dry.

2. Boil the chicken in just enough lightly salted water for an hour. Drain and set aside to cool. When it is cool enough de-bone the chicken into pieces but keep the skin on. Reserve the cooking water.

3. In a large pan warm the butter over medium heat. Add the crushed garlic and dried coriander and cook, stirring frequently, for 3 minutes.

4. Add the Molokhia and cook, stirring, for another 3 to 4 minutes,

5. Add the chicken, lemon juice, salt, pepper and paprika. Stir well. Cover and cook over medium heat for 45 minutes, or until thickened. From time to time check to see if the mixture is too dry and you need to add some of the reserved chicken cooking water. If you prefer the malokhia to be wetter, add more liquid, if you prefer it drier add less or no extra liquid.

6. Serve with rice.

Rice Pudding

Halawet el Jibn (Sweet Cheese)

"This is a popular, traditional Syrian sweet that came from Hama. My family has adopted it as our own. We have it on days when we have larger meals and always when we have company. This is a treat for after a meal. My mother made this when I was growing up and now, I make it for my children."

Ingredients

1 kg Akkawi cheese
(mozzarella also works well)
3 tbsp (45 ml) rose water
1 cup (200 g) sugar
1 cup (250 ml) water
1 kg fine semolina

For the cream filling

1 litre fresh cream
80 g cornflour
80 ml water

For the syrup

2 cups (400 g) sugar
2 cups (500 ml) water

To garnish

pistachio nuts
lemon blossoms

What To Do

1. To make the cream filling: add the water to a saucepan and dissolve the cornflour. Stir in the cream and bring to the boil. Reduce the heat and stir constantly until the cream has thickened. Set aside to cool

2. Slice the cheese into small cubes and place in a dish. Note: you can skip the soaking if you are using mozzarella cheese. Add enough cold water to cover and soak in the refrigerator overnight. Change the water several times to get rid of the excess salt, using fresh cold water each time. Drain well when done.

3. Add the cheese and rose water to a non-stick saucepan on low heat. Stir constantly until the cheese has melted. Remove the pan from the heat and set aside. Discard any water that has separated from the cheese.

4. Add the water and sugar to a pot on medium heat and stir occasionally until the sugar has dissolved. Add the cheese and stir in with a wooden spoon. When the cheese has melted, gradually add the semolina until you get a consistent dough. Remove from the heat and set aside to cool. When it is cool enough to handle knead the dough for a minute to get a smooth consistency. Divide the dough in 2.

5. Lay a sheet of cling film on the counter top. Roll the dough into a rectangle about 5 mm thick. Trim the edges to neaten. Pipe or spread a line of filling across the dough, about 1 cm in from the bottom edge. Carefully roll the dough over until the filling is covered. Slice across the dough to separate the roll and repeat until the dough is used up. Place each roll a tray lined with cling film. Repeat with the second batch of dough. Place the tray in the fridge for two hours fir the rolls to firm up before cutting.

6. When the dough is firm, slice the rolls into pieces, either cutting straight across or at an angle.

7. To serve, garnish with pistachios and lemon blossoms and the cooled sugar syrup.

To make the sugar syrup:

8. Into a saucepan add the water and sugar and bring to the boil. Stir until the sugar has dissolved completely.

9. Add the juice of 1/2 lemon and reduce the heat. Simmer for 10 minutes until syrupy.

Rice Pudding

Ingredients

1 litre whole milk
250g pudding rice, soaked in hot water for 10 minutes
1 tbsp (13 g) sugar
1 tsp (5 ml) rosewater
1 tsp (5 ml) vanilla extract
1 tsp (5 g) cornflour
desiccated coconut to garnish (optional)

What To Do

1. In a medium-sized saucepan set over medium-high heat, bring the milk to the boil.

2. Just before the milk boils, add the rice, reduce the heat to medium and cook, constantly stirring, for 15 minutes.

3. Add sugar, rosewater, vanilla and corn starch. Lower the heat and stir frequently. Cook for another 15 minutes, or until rice is cooked.

4. Spoon into small bowls and top with coconut (optional).

Baklava

"Baklava is well known in Syria, Turkey and throughout the Middle East. This sweet is particularly popular at special times. When a man wants to marry a woman, it is customary for his family to send a delegation of representatives to the woman's home to ask for her family's permission to wed. They will usually bring gifts, including huge plates (5 to 7 kgs) of baklava! My sister-in-law taught me how to make it. In Syria, homemade filo is typically used, but in England I buy the pastry readymade, which makes the recipe much quicker and easier to prepare."

Ingredients

For the Baklava

1 (40 sheet) packet filo pastry, thawed if frozen
250 g butter or margarine
1 cup (250 ml) vegetable oil
150 g unsalted, shelled pistachio nuts

For the Syrup

3 cups (750 ml) water
3 cups (600 g) sugar
juice of 1/2 lemon

To garnish

crushed pistachio nuts or desiccated coconut

What To Do

1. Prepare the filling before cutting the filo pastry to size as it dries very quickly. Keep it covered with a slightly damp tea towel.

2. In a small saucepan set over low heat melt the butter. Remove from the heat and stir in the oil. Set aside.

3. Place the pistachios in a food processor and pulse several times to crush into small pieces. Set aside.

4. Preheat the oven to 200° C.

5. You can use a round or square/rectangular non-stick baking pan about 20 – 25 cm wide. Divide the pastry into two stacks of 20 sheets each and cover with a slightly damp tea towel. Place the baking pan upside down on top of a stack of 20 filo sheets trim the filo to size. Repeat with the second stack. Cover the pastry with a slightly damp tea towel so it doesn't dry out.

6. Brush the bottom and sides of the baking pan with butter, making sure you get right into the corners.

7. To assemble the baklava: place a filo square or disc on a flat, clean worksurface and brush with the butter/oil mixture. Place another sheet on top and again brush with butter/oil mix. Repeat with the remaining filo discs/squares. Place the stack into the baking pan. Spread the nuts on top.

8. Brush the remaining stack of filo the same way and place into the baking pan.

9. Use a sharp knife to cut through the filo layers in parallel lines to make diamond shaped pieces.

10. Bake for 20 - 25 minutes in the preheated oven, or until the filo is golden and crisp.

11. While the baklava is baking make the syrup. Add the water and sugar to a saucepan on medium heat and bring to the boil, stirring occasionally. When the liquid starts to bubble, stir in the lemon juice. Simmer for 10 minutes, or until the liquid becomes syrupy. Remove from the heat and set aside to cool to room temperature.

12. Once the baklava has finished baking, remove it from the oven and pour over the syrup to drench the filo. Set aside to cool.

13. Serve sprinkled with crushed pistachios or desiccated coconut.

Harissa Semolina Cake

Ingredients

3 cups (560 g) semolina, medium ground
1 cup (200 g) sugar
1/2 tsp (2 g) baking powder
2 tbsp (30 g) powdered milk
50 g ghee
2 cups (500 ml) sugar syrup
1 cup (250 ml) warm water
1 tbsp (20 g) tahini (sesame paste)
160 g pistachios, roughly chopped

What To Do

1. In a large bowl mix the semolina, sugar and baking powder. Add the powdered milk and rub the ingredients together by hand.

2. Add the ghee and 1 cup of sugar syrup and mix well. Add the water and mix until all the ingredients are well incorporated.

3. Grease a medium-sized baking tray with tahini using a brush. Spread the semolina mixture evenly in the tray and smooth the surface.

4. Cover the tray with foil and set aside for 2 hours.

5. Preheat the oven to 180 ° C.

6. Remove the foil and spread the pistachios evenly over the batter.

7. Bake for 20 minutes, or until the surface is golden brown.

8. Pour the remaining cup of sugar syrup evenly over top and allow to cool before serving.

Ma'amoul

"This is a very famous cookie that is usually made in festive times and for celebrations. It was served at my wedding. When my children get married, I want to make sure that we serve this cookie at their weddings too."

Ingredients

5 cups (600 g) plain flour
1 tbsp (12 g) baking powder
1 cup (240 g) butter, softened
1 cup (250 ml) corn oil
1 cup (250 ml) milk

For the date paste

1/2 kg dates, made to paste
1 tbsp (15 ml) rose water
1 tbsp (15 g) butter, softened
2 tbsp desiccated coconut (optional)

What To Do

1. To make the date paste put all the ingredients into a mixing bowl and knead with your hands until the mixture is well combined. Cut into small pieces to be used as filling.

2. In a large bowl, whisk together the flour and baking powder.

3. Add to the jug of a blender the milk, butter, oil, and milk and blend until creamy.

4. Pour the mixture into the bowl with flour and stir until you have a soft and smooth dough.

5. Take a small piece of dough and make a dip in the middle. Place a bit of the date paste filling inside the dip and seal it well. Place it into a ma'amoul press (you can find these online) and squeeze to form. Repeat with the remaining dough.

6. Preheat the oven to 200 ° C.

7. Grease a baking tray with butter and arrange the ma'amoul on it.

8. Bake in the pre-heated oven for 30 – 40 minutes, or until golden brown.

9. Set aside to cool before storing them in an airtight container.

46

47

White Cheese Pies

Ingredients

For the filling

1 cup (130 g) white cheese (ideally Czech Akkawi)
1/2 cup (22 g) parsley, chopped
1 egg, beaten
1 tbsp (15 g) butter (or margarine), softened

For the dough

1 cup (250 ml) warm water
1 tsp (5 g) sugar
1 tsp (5 g) salt
1 tsp (4 g) dry active yeast
3 cups (360 g) plain flour
1/4 cup (63 ml) vegetable oil

What To Do

1. First, prepare the filling. Grate the cheese and put it in a bowl. Add the parsley and mix. Beat in the egg. Then beat in the butter (or margarine) until all the ingredients are well mixed. Set aside.

2. In a large bowl, thoroughly mix the water, yeast and sugar together.

3. Sieve the flour into another bowl, add the yeast mixture and the oil. Mix well until you get a dough. Knead the dough well using your hands, then cover and allow to rest for about 15 minutes.

4. Roll the dough out on a lightly-floured board. Cut into oval shaped pieces. Put about one tablespoon of filling, just off-centre, into each parcel. Pull the edge over and seal the edges well using your fingertips.

5. Preheat the oven to 200°C.

6. Brush an oven tray with oil and arrange the parcels on it.

7. Bake for 15 - 20 minutes, or until golden brown.

Most of the ingredients in this book can be sourced from local supermarkets. However, the more specialist ingredients can be purchased at any Turkish food shop. There are six branches of Turkish Food Centre (TFC) across North London and the families always go there for their grocery shopping. There are also many Arabic grocery stores near Edgware Road. A specific shop for Syrian food is Damas Gate - 81 Uxbridge Rd, White City, London W12 8NR.